This book belongs to:
AF374165

THE BABY HEART DOCTOR

A Notable Black Hero Who Saved Babies From "Blue Baby Syndrome"

Written by June Williams-Newton

Illustrated by Brittany Lewis-Moore

The Baby Heart Doctor
A Black Hero Who Saved Babies From "Blue Baby Syndrome"

Written By June Williams-Newton
Illustrated by Brittany Lewis-Moore

Published by June Williams-Newton

Mary Esther, Florida

Library of Congress Control Number: 2023915060

Printed in the United States of America
ISBN: 979-8-9885611-0-1

Self-Publishing Services by DG Self-Publishing
www.dgselfpublishing.com

Table of Contents

NOTEWORTHY

Many notable Black heroes have made a distinguishable mark on the world. These individuals did not set out to become heroes but were given a chance somewhere in their growing lives to make their talents flourish—all during a time when life was very hard for Black people.

They were not viewed as important, nor did they receive good treatment in society. For instance, they did not have the freedom to go to certain schools or have good jobs like White people did.

In this case, Vivien Thomas achieved remarkable and respectable status as a surgeon, making a difference by saving babies with Blue Baby Syndrome—a condition which caused the babies' skin to literally turn blue due to oxygen being blocked from reaching their little hearts.

The story of Vivien Thomas demonstrates how even if boundaries and obstacles are met in life, they can be overcome—by anyone.

This book can be read to much younger children, but be sure to stop and explain the content to help them understand.

CHAPTER 1
WHO WAS VIVIEN THOMAS?

Vivien Thomas was born on August 29, 1910, in Lake Providence, Louisiana.

During that time, life in Louisiana was not like it is today. Many things we have today did not exist when Vivien was growing up. There were very few cars and trucks, most people had no televisions, and definitely no computers or cell phones.

Also, there were no grocery stores, so people got their food from small shops or grew vegetables and fruits and raised animals. This is called farming. It was the way of life, and because of it, people spent a lot of time outside.

Some of the plants the farmers grew were cotton and sugarcane, which were their main crops. From sugarcane, they made sugar and syrup. It can also be eaten as a snack—it is juicy, like a pineapple, and very sweet. With cotton, they created products like sheets, curtains, rugs, and fabric to make clothes.

Sugarcane as a snack—the juice comes out as you bite into it

Cotton Farm

The forests were an important resource because of the large amount of wood the trees supplied. Many items were built with wood, such as tables, chairs, and doors. The wood supply also helped to build some houses. Unlike today, houses were mostly built entirely of wood.

There were very few cars when Vivien was growing up, so people traveled by horse and carriage or carts. A carriage is made up of four wheels and pulled by one or more horses, while a smaller cart usually has two wheels and can be pulled by a single horse. Other forms of transportation included trains and even by boat through waterways.

Vivien's dad was a carpenter. Carpenters build things made of wood, like tables, chairs, beds, cabinets, houses, horse carriages, horse carts, and many other items from wood. Often, he chopped and gathered his own wood by going into the forest and hauled it to his workshop.

Horse Carriage

Horse Cart

Vivien's dad had all the tools necessary to build any item he wanted. He also fixed broken wooden items, bringing them back into good condition. Vivien's dad worked with wood for many years and became very good at his craft. For that reason, he was known as a master carpenter. That means he was an expert!

Vivien began working for his dad at the young age of seven. He spent his time helping out with woodworking jobs by gathering the wood and tools for cutting and shaping the wood.

He was taught how to carefully handle and use sharp tools, as some of them were dangerous. He learned how to measure wood and safely operate the big machines to do the cutting all on his own.

Woodworking tools

Years later, his family moved to Nashville, Tennessee, where Vivien attended public school. He got outstanding scores in all his classes because he was smart. And because he was smart, he raised his hand a lot to answer questions.

Unfortunately, Vivien's parents were very poor, so they didn't have enough money to send him to college.

When he was a teenager and started high school, he continued working with his dad to earn money. Vivien saved all of it to help pay for his college education after he finished high school.

However, when Vivien was ready to go to college, he soon discovered the money he saved was not enough. So, he looked for jobs where he could make more money.

CHAPTER 2
GETTING MORE WORK

In Tennessee, Vivien found work as a janitor at Vanderbilt University. As a janitor, his duties were to clean the floors and take out the trash.

In this college was a large laboratory. This was a room where doctors and scientists performed research by examining animals to observe how they could fix whatever was wrong with them. There were tables to work on and a lot of different tools and machines used to explore and examine experiments.

This was where Vivien met his mentor, Doctor Alfred Blalock. Doctor Blalock worked in a laboratory where he studied dogs.

He performed surgeries on the dogs' hearts to find out why they were sick and to figure out ways to make them well. He mostly worked on dogs because the parts of a dog's heart are much like a human's.

Oftentimes, when Vivien noticed Doctor Blalock going into the laboratory, he wondered what the doctor was doing inside.

Luckily for Vivien, there was a glass window for him to peer inside. One day, he was very curious and decided to peek through, but the window was too high and he could not get a glimpse of what the doctor was up to. So, he grabbed a nearby chair and stood on it to watch what was going on.

Through the window, Vivien saw dogs lying on metal tables, and they all looked like they were sleeping.

He also noticed a lot of tools like knives and other metal objects on other tables.

The lights hanging from their poles shined brightly above Doctor Blalock's operating tables.

One day, Doctor Blalock saw Vivien peeking in the window. Fascinated by his curiosity, he invited Vivien into the laboratory, which allowed Vivien to observe Doctor Blalock's medical practices. Since Vivien now had the advantage of watching up close, he began to understand what was happening.

The doctor explained the procedure to Vivien, starting with how he injected the sick dogs with medicine to put them to sleep, or as medical professionals would call it, under anesthesia, so they would not feel pain while they had surgery on their hearts.

After some time, Doctor Blalock asked Vivien to help him in the lab.

He taught Vivien how to use the medical tools and how to move the dogs around on the table to make precise cuts during surgery. Doctor Blalock was very glad to have him in the laboratory. Vivien was good at following instructions, and since he was a quick learner, Doctor Blalock made Vivien his assistant so he could help with the experiments.

Before the dogs received sleep injections, Vivien helped to weigh them on a scale to determine how strong their injection medicine should be.

Vivien Thomas and assistants operating on a laboratory dog

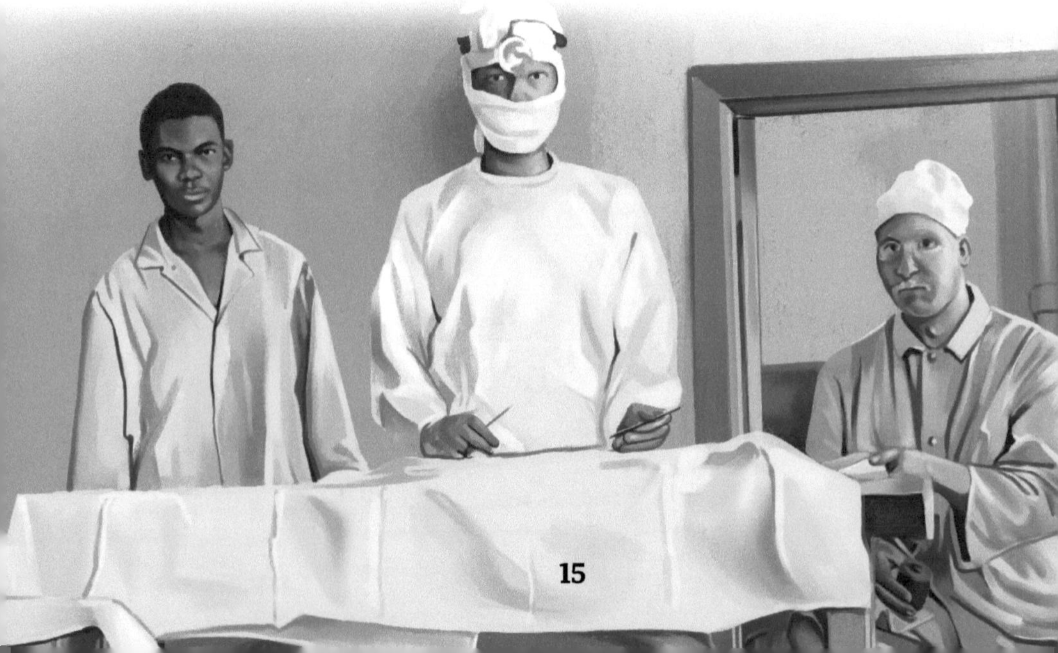

The bigger dogs received a larger amount of medicine than the smaller dogs. Within days, Vivien was responsible for giving the dogs injections all by himself. That became his job, and he was very good at it.

Since Vivien showed exceptional skills in the laboratory, he was trusted to work alone without anyone telling him what to do. Eventually, Vivien became the laboratory manager. His job was to keep the laboratory in good working condition by cleaning the tools and making sure they were stored away correctly when experiments or surgeries were complete.

CHAPTER 3
GREAT WORKER

Even though he worked helping Doctor Blalock in the laboratory, Vivien was still a janitor. Most of the other Black people who worked at Vanderbilt University were also janitors. In those times, Black people's jobs usually involved cleaning duties.

Although he worked long hours in the laboratory, he was not paid the same as the White people who worked there. In fact, he got paid very little money because he was a Black man.

Vivien knew he should receive more money for his hard work. So, one day, he asked Doctor Blalock for an increase in pay because of all his great work. Doctor Blalock agreed, and that's when Vivien began to receive the same amount of money as his White coworkers.

Vivien handled the laboratory tools carefully. The way he made cutting incisions with scissors and tied knots was splendid. He was so talented at handling medical instruments that Doctor Blalock thought he was ready to become a laboratory technician. As a laboratory technician, he got to teach other people what to do in the laboratory and give help.

Vivien loved working with the dogs and performing heart surgeries. After many months, he designed new surgery tools and taught, or trained, other doctors how to use them.

The doctors and technicians liked that Vivien was smart and hardworking. This was remarkable for anyone, even more so for a Black man who never went to college or medical school. Vivien was not a doctor but showed a natural talent for medical practice.

CHAPTER 4
BLUE BABY SYNDROME

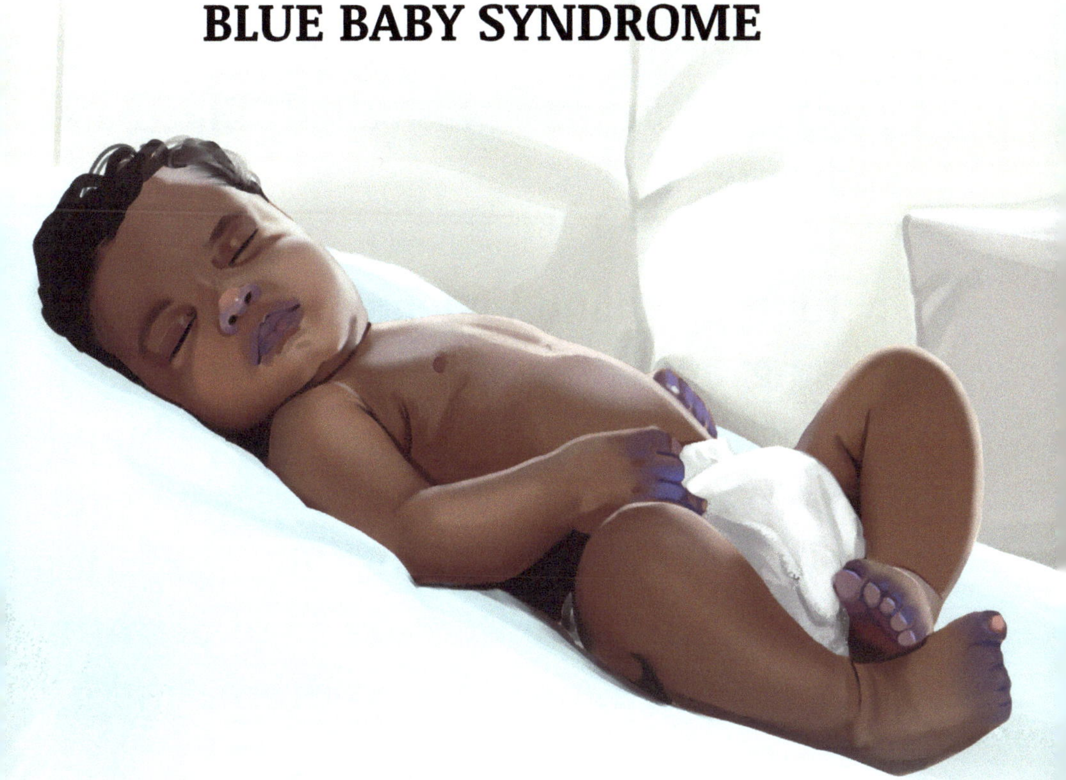

Back in those days, doctors discovered babies born with too little oxygen or air moving in their blood. When blood does not have enough oxygen, it turns blue, which causes the babies' lips and skin to appear blue.

This meant the pathways that carried blood and oxygen back and forth from the heart to the lungs were blocked. When that happened, it prevented oxygen from going into the blood. Without enough oxygen going into the blood, their lungs received a low amount of blood which caused them to be sick. The sickness was called "Blue Baby Syndrome."

Doctor Blalock and Vivien spent a long time studying and practicing surgery on dog hearts while trying to learn how to get blood to flow through the lungs properly. After they had performed almost 200 surgeries on dog hearts, they were ready to perform operations for Blue Baby Syndrome and fix the hearts of babies.

Healthy Baby Heart

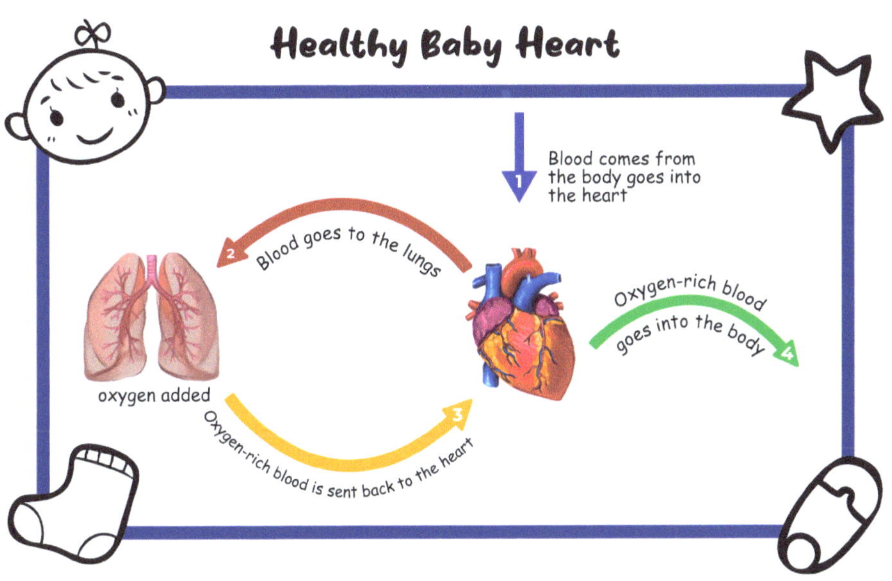

Sick Blue Baby Heart

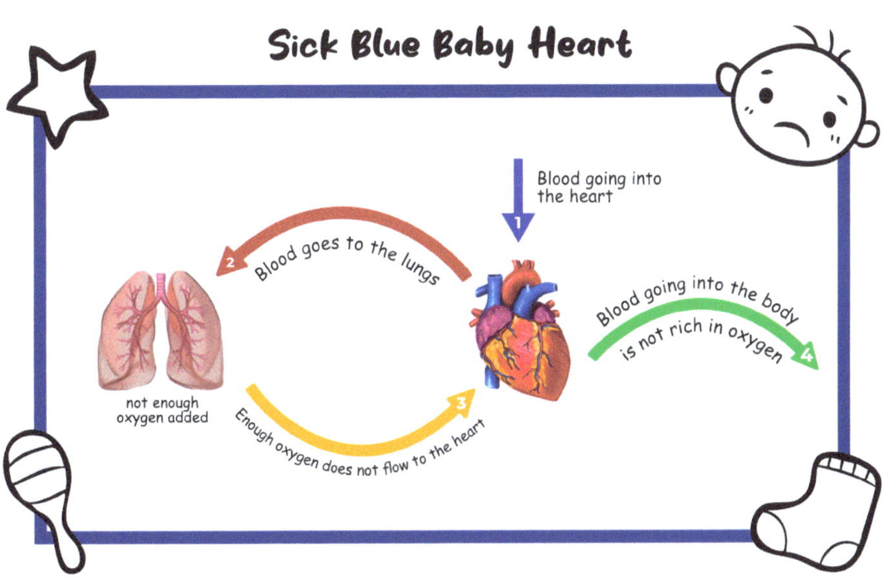

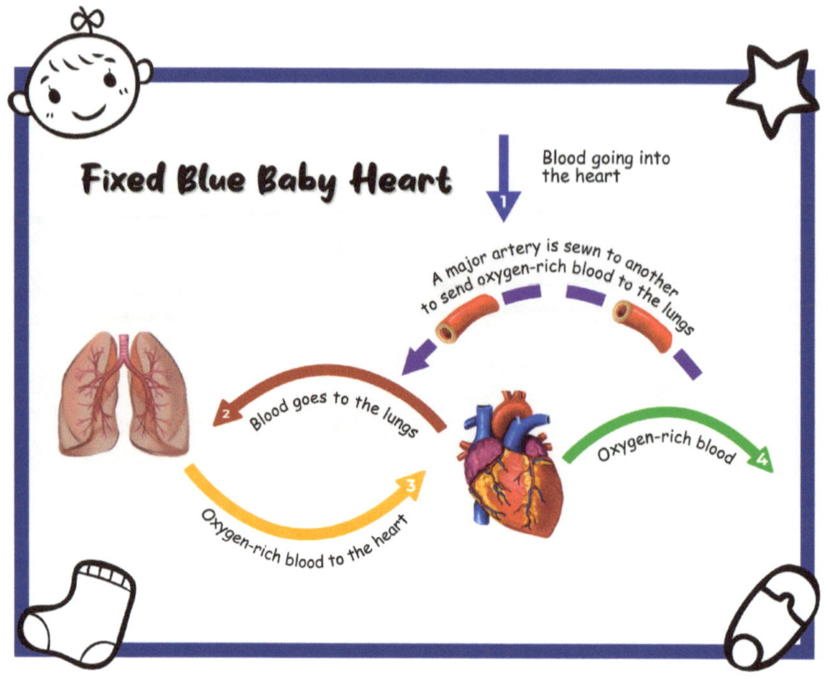

They worked together to develop detailed surgery techniques to solve the heart problem because they realized they needed to create a new procedure to allow for proper oxygen and blood flow to the heart and lungs. This new procedure divided a major artery and sewed it into another artery that would send the blood directly to the lungs, which made a new pathway for oxygen to flow from the heart to the lungs! Hooray!

CHAPTER 5
MIRACLE HEART TEAM

Years later, Doctor Blalock's work moved to a Baltimore, Maryland hospital called Johns Hopkins Hospital. He knew how well Vivien worked and trusted him enough to keep working together, so he asked Vivien to move with him to Baltimore.

By now Vivien had a family: a wife and two daughters. It meant leaving the home they had built in Nashville for a strange city and an uncertain future, but he was happy to go along to work with Doctor Blalock in the new city and, even more exciting, in a new laboratory, and so, Vivien made the move.

Baltimore proved to be more expensive to live in than Nashville, and Vivien's salary was not enough to support his family of four. It was unfortunate that his salary was decided before he left Nashville, so an increase in his salary was not possible.

However, Doctor Blalock reached out to a friend, known for his generosity, who made a donation towards Vivien's salary. With that increase, he was able to order supplies he needed for his work.

Since Doctor Blalock had a lot of trust in Vivien, he wanted him to manage the surgery laboratory. Like his job before, this new job was also to take care of and keep count of the supplies they used for surgeries.

As laboratory manager, he prepared for surgeries by checking every tool used and making sure they were ready and clean.

He also had to be sure the equipment used for surgeries was cleaned and put away after the surgeries. Vivien did his job as laboratory manager for thirty-five years.

The Vanderbilt staff was surprised that Doctor Blalock brought a Black man to run his laboratory, and even more surprised that he was not even a doctor!

As Vivien walked down the dimly lit hallways of Johns Hopkins, he eyeballed how creepy the place looked with bare concrete floors and paint peeling off the walls. His breath was taken away when he saw an old space that was supposed to be his workplace. It was enough to give him a nudge to head back to Nashville and take up his carpenter's tools again, but he didn't.

At the new job in Maryland, Vivien met another doctor, Denton Cooley, who was impressed by how Vivien did surgeries, and thought he made the job of doing surgery look very easy.

They became good friends and soon developed a plan to be workmates in the laboratory. Together they performed operations that would save the "blue babies." Doctor Cooley and other surgeons gave credit to Vivien for teaching them the techniques of the operations that made them famous in the field of medicine.

At Johns Hopkins Hospital, Vivien walked around in a white laboratory coat that was given to him for work: the same kind the doctors wore.

On his first walk-through, the people working at the hospital stopped and stared at Vivien, a Black man, as he flew through the hallways in his white coat. Their eyes grew wide in amazement when they discovered a Black man was managing the laboratory.

Inside the laboratory, technicians who worked there were also very amazed at seeing how well he worked. They had never seen him doing surgery. They thought his job was to set up the equipment and tools for surgery. Vivien's actions were such a surprise to them, that the other doctors wondered how long he had been doing surgeries, and they wanted to know where he learned how.

After a while, the fact Vivien was a Black man working in the laboratory didn't matter because of how good he was at doing surgeries. He was now a part of the team who worked together to do great things that would impact medical history forever!

CHAPTER 6
SAVING A LIFE

On November 29, 1944, Doctor Blalock got a chance to do an operation on an actual person, a baby girl who showed signs of Blue Baby Syndrome. Her skin was deeply blue, and her lips and nails were purple. This operation aimed to get enough oxygen into the blood so that more blood could travel to her lungs.

Although Vivien did not go to college and therefore was not a formally educated doctor, Doctor Blalock insisted Vivien stand on a step stool behind him to offer help while doing the surgeries. After all, Vivien had done the procedure dozens of times.

He was not allowed to do operations on humans, but he could help by looking over Doctor Blalock's shoulder to answer questions.

The surgery to fix a situation where the blood does not get enough oxygen to flow to the lungs was considered impossible, but Vivien and Doctor Blalock had lots of experience with dogs who had the same condition, so they knew exactly what to do.

The operation on the baby girl was successful. Her sickly, blue-colored skin went away, and her skin color went back to normal, meaning there was enough oxygen flowing in her blood from her heart to her lungs.

A lot of Vivien's work was to teach other doctors how to perform the appropriate surgeries. They did them fast and without wasting time or making mistakes.

Although Vivien grew up poor, he got a big chance in life. He was lucky to be working in those laboratories because a hospital was not a place for a Black person to work as a doctor back then, even if he did go to college.

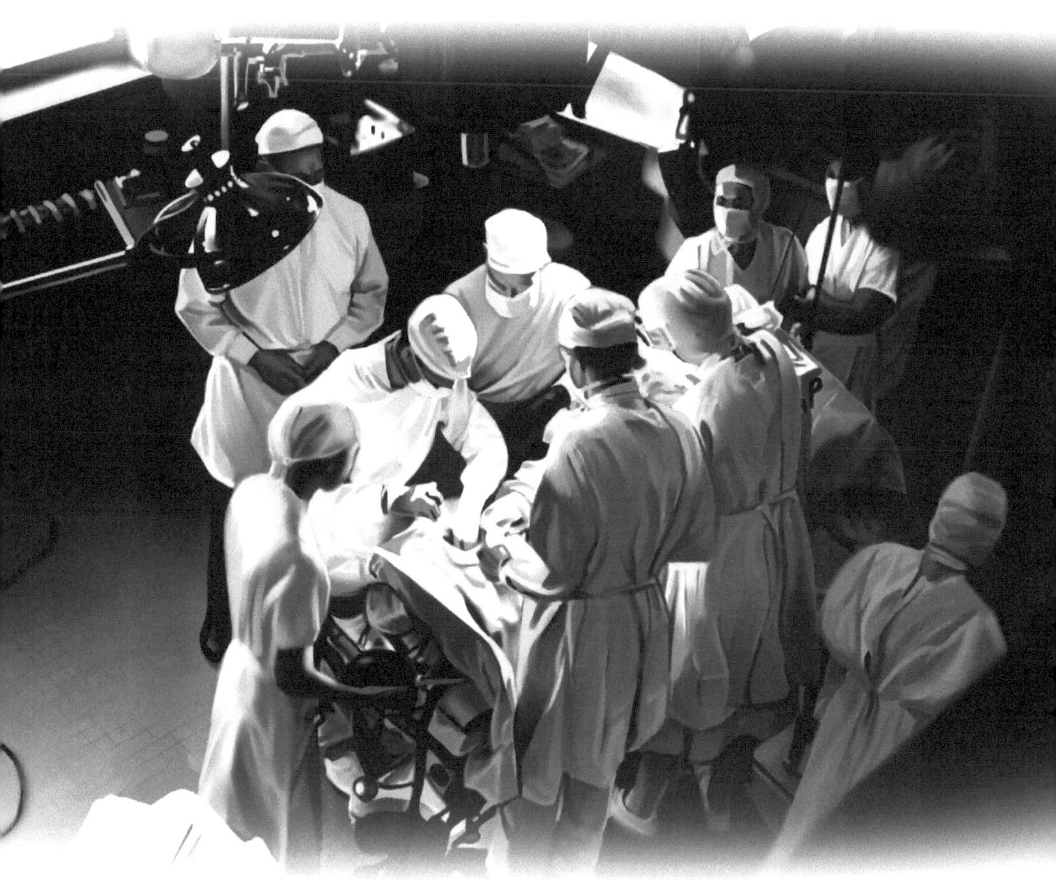

Vivien stands behind Doctor Blalock (behind lamp) giving instructions in surgery

In his accomplishments, Vivien also designed his own surgical equipment since no specialized tools existed for operating on infant hearts.

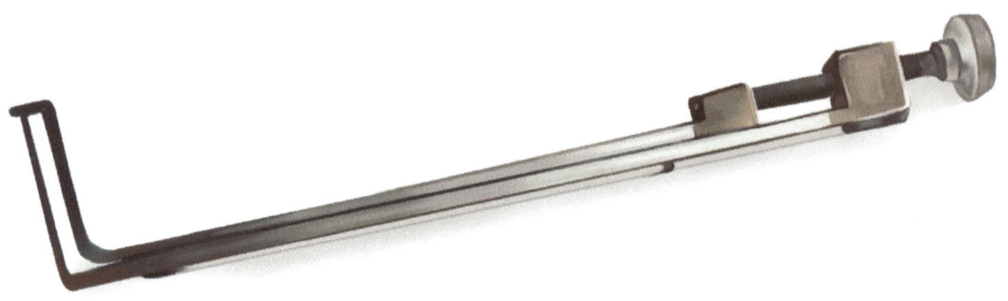

Clamp Vivien Thomas helped create for the temporary closure of the artery

The infants' blood vessels were too small for the surgical equipment they used, so Vivien created the idea to cut needles down shorter and sharper and created a new clamp to use on the tiny arteries. He worked to develop another clamp for temporarily closing the artery of the heart that went to the lungs, which allowed doctors to stop the bleeding in their little chests during these special surgeries.

Doctor Blalock valued Vivien's work and tried to help him have a fulfilling career, but he didn't give him credit for all his work. They made important discoveries during their years of surgery, but only Doctor Blalock was recognized. It wasn't known that Vivien was such a great worker with heart surgeries.

Vivien Thomas created something special with his skillful hands and brilliant mind that saved the lives of many babies with Blue Baby Syndrome.

CHAPTER 7
FROM POOR TO PIONEER

News of this captivating story of the surgery spread around the world and made Doctor Blalock famous as a hero. Before this, he was seen as a rebel by some of the people he worked with because he was known to yell and knock things down when he got angry.

Vivien's involvement was unacknowledged by Doctor Blalock and the Johns Hopkins School of Medicine. They did not spread the word that Vivien was a big part of the new surgery discovery.

Within one year, the surgery procedure was used to resolve Blue Baby Syndrome in more than 200 patients at the Johns Hopkins School of Medicine. This led to dozens of parents bringing their sick children from many miles away.

In 1976, Johns Hopkins School of Medicine awarded Vivien an honorary doctorate degree. That means, without going to college, he was given a college degree for his hard and dedicated work. From then on, he was called Doctor Vivien Thomas. They also named him an instructor of surgery because he taught the surgical procedures and was able to teach many doctors who would go on to have big important jobs like chiefs of surgery in many hospitals across the country.

Vivien rose above being poor and treated unfairly to being an expert in cardiac surgery and a great teacher who was respected by many of the country's best doctors.

MORAL OF VIVIEN THOMAS' STORY:

This is a lesson about perseverance and hard work. Hard work and dedication are important if you want to get ahead. The obstacles of being poor and Black did not stop Vivien from working hard, even in times when Black people were not usually treated well. Being an awesome worker for his dad prepared him to be a skillful worker for Doctor Blalock. Having discipline and a good work ethic will help you to be ready for great opportunities and difficulties that may come your way. Also, at times, life isn't fair, but you have to work through the difficulties to become successful.

ABOUT THE AUTHOR

June Williams-Newton is a mother, wife, and retired United States Air Force veteran. She is also the grandmother to two smart, talented, and awesome "grandcuties!"

She loves to meditate daily and sometimes has her matcha green tea in a ceremonial meditative "locus" for enlightenment! This brings her from great "head" to great "body". As she sees it, God gave her only one body, and she shows appreciation by working out regularly and eating wisely.

June has done a plethora of writing throughout her career. As a veteran, she wrote many publications and rulebooks, as well as numerous performance reports. She even writes a Happiness blog, which she created to help ignite a passion to write more while getting people to pitch into 'happiness.'

Post-military, she has been a personal fitness trainer, Zumba instructor, and substitute teacher. But it was while teaching in elementary schools that she discovered a majority of biographies about Black people were of athletes and historical figures. Primarily individuals who were already familiar to the public, like Martin Luther King and Rosa Parks. June knew there were more Black figures like Vivien Thomas that readers could learn about.

After seeing an impressive movie, she realized there was a remarkable Black historical figure to write about. The movie on the life of Vivien Thomas drove June to do her part in exposing the great contributions he made to this world, more specifically, the medical industry.

SHARE YOUR FEEDBACK!

Did you enjoy this book? Please post a review on Amazon to let others know about your experience. Your review will help with getting this book into the hands of more children, and we would love to hear your feedback!

www.ingramcontent.com/pod-product-compliance
Lightning Source LLC
Chambersburg PA
CBHW040901110726
48005CB00001B/146